W9-CAF-828

BE A FRIEND
Children Who Live with HIV Speak

Art and Writing
Compiled by
Lori S. Wiener, Ph.D.
Aprille Best
Philip A. Pizzo, M.D.

Foreword by
Robert Coles

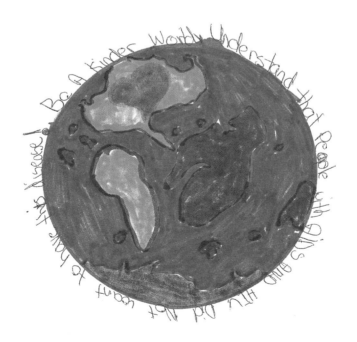

ALBERT WHITMAN & COMPANY
Morton Grove, Illinois

To children and families whose lives have been,
and will be, affected by HIV.

*To my own family, who unknowingly walked into the world of AIDS
and whose lives have been so greatly affected by this disease,
thank you for remaining at my side through this journey and for
providing me with such safe arms to come home to. L.S.W.*

For Ezra. A.B.

Lori S. Wiener, Ph.D., a clinical social worker,
is Coordinator, Pediatric HIV
Psychosocial Support Program, National Cancer Institute,
National Institutes of Health, Bethesda, MD.

Aprille Best is an artist who lost her son, Ezra, to AIDS.

Philip A. Pizzo, M.D., is Chief of Pediatrics and Head,
Infectious Disease Section, National Cancer Institute.

All profits and royalties from this book will be donated
to the Pediatric AIDS Foundation.

Library of Congress Cataloging-in-Publication Data

Be a friend: children who live with HIV speak / art and writing compiled by
Lori S. Wiener, Aprille Best, Philip A. Pizzo; foreword by Robert Coles.
p. cm.
ISBN 0-8075-0590-0
1. AIDS (Disease) in children—Patients—Miscellanea—Juvenile literature.
(1. AIDS (Disease)—Patients. 2. Children's writings. 3. Children's art.)
I. Wiener, Lori S. II. Best, Aprille. III. Pizzo, Philip A.
RJ387.A25B4   1994   93-29595
362.1'98929792—dc20   CIP   AC

Copyright © 1994 by Albert Whitman & Company.
Published in 1994 by Albert Whitman & Company,
6340 Oakton Street, Morton Grove, IL 60053.
Published simultaneously in Canada by General Publishing, Limited, Toronto.
All rights reserved. No part of this book may be reproduced or transmitted in any form or by
any means, electronic or mechanical, including photocopying, recording, or by any
information storage and retrieval system, without permission in writing from the publisher.
Printed in the United States of America.
10 9 8 7 6 5 4 3 2 1

No endorsement of any product or publication of Albert Whitman & Company is made by
either the National Cancer Institute or the authors through the publication of this work.

Book design by Susan B. Cohn.
Cover collage by Eileen Mueller Neill.
Text set in Lemonade Bold and Avant Garde Book.

FOREWORD

In the pages that follow we learn of the remarkable capacity children have to tell themselves, to tell others, exactly what is happening—remarkable because so many of us who are grown up have learned quite other ways of thinking and feeling: the strategies of deception and self-deception, of evasion and contradiction, which, alas, inform so much of our everyday lives. For these boys and girls, life may be short, may even be, to draw upon the well-known Hobbesian categorization, mean and brutish (that is, full of hurt and pain). Yet there is no surrender to that major temptation of self-pity or bitterness, each of which is an aspect of despair. Rather, these children, afflicted with a disease that unfortunately now promises, eventually, to take their lives, ask questions, speculate, turn to moral, philosophical, and spiritual reflection. In a sense the words and pictures that follow affirm the rock-bottom humanity of the young speakers and writers, the artists. Already they know that there is an end to things; already they contemplate and scrutinize this world, think of what is fair and unfair, just and unjust, and hope (hope against hope), even when the odds are highly unfavorable, indeed. It is a privilege then—an inspiration, too—for the rest of us (not without our own reasons to look at the world, to search for answers to life's great challenges and mysteries) to meet these wonderfully alert, sensitive, thoughtful fellow pilgrims, who have so very much to tell about how to live this life, how to try to understand it, no matter the trials that have come their way.

Robert Coles

INTRODUCTION

As of June 1993, 4,710 children in this country had been diagnosed as having AIDS (Acquired Immune Deficiency Syndrome), a disease caused by the human immunodeficiency virus (HIV). Because HIV harms the body's immune system (its natural ability to fight illness), the body becomes susceptible to serious infections and even cancer.

Many more children in America do not yet have AIDS, but have been infected by HIV. They will eventually get AIDS. And throughout the world, millions of children and adults now have AIDS or are infected with HIV. The number is increasing rapidly, and, unfortunately, at present there is no cure.

Since 1986, over 350 children with AIDS or HIV infection have come to the National Cancer Institute in Bethesda, Maryland, where they can be treated by medicines being developed to fight HIV. Often these medicines are so new that they may not be available elsewhere. While undergoing treatment, each child also meets with a social worker. The staff of the NCI believe that children need more than medicine to fight the virus. They benefit greatly when given the opportunity to express their feelings.

Some young patients give form to their feelings through play with dolls and puppets and through storytelling. Others draw pictures and write stories to make their own "books," adding a new "chapter" on each return visit. Brothers and sisters can also make their own books.

Be a Friend is a collection of art and writing by children who have come to the National Cancer Institute. It is divided into three sections. In "I Often Wonder . . .," children express what they wonder about and wish for: for example, what life would be like without AIDS; how sick they will get; if they will die; and, if so, what heaven will be like.

For many children, there are frequent visits to a hospital clinic, needle sticks, daily medications, and periods of feeling ill. In "Living with HIV," these children speak of their desire just to be "normal." They also imagine what HIV might look like, creating fierce monsters as well as having fantasies about becoming friends with the virus and fighting a war together.

HIV can be a chronic disease, and some children can go for months or years without serious problems. For these children, the virus is not the central concern. Instead, they worry about what will happen if they tell people they have HIV. Will they still have friends?

Part of living with HIV is knowing one can die. All children want to be remembered, and they worry about how their families will cope when they are gone. Children also think a lot about heaven and life after death. Most are not very frightened of dying itself. Their fears are of the actual separation from their friends and loved ones. We see these concerns, too, in "Living with HIV."

The siblings of sick children worry about their brothers' and sisters' illness and feel the strain of keeping the family's secret. They may feel lonely or angry because the sick child gets everyone's attention. Other children, themselves ill, speak of missing parents and friends who have died of AIDS. But both sick children and their siblings long for understanding. In the words of one child, "Please do not be scared of us. . . . We need you to be our friends." These issues are explored in "Family, Friends, and AIDS."

Each child has had a different experience in accepting illness and being accepted by others, and each has been able to face his or her fears with courage and clarity. In compiling this book, it was difficult to choose from among so many deeply felt and powerfully expressed hopes and fears.

Several of the children whose work is produced in this book have died since the project began. Jeremy, Ricky, Becky, Sara—as I promised, your words will live on forever. For the rest of you, I can only hope that through this book, you will touch others' lives as much as you have touched mine.

Lori S. Wiener, Ph.D.
Coordinator, Pediatric HIV Pychosocial Support Program,
National Cancer Institute

I often wonder . . .

. . . why I have to get shots.
. . . if I am going to get sick.
. . . why *my mommy* died.

Cassie, age 5

DEAR GOD,

    I often wonder where you came from. How did you get all of your magic power? Why did we have to get AIDS? Where did it come from? Do you have a cure for AIDS? If you do, please, we need it now. But if you can't, can you make the Yankees and White Sox and the Cubs win the World Series?

Love,

Joey, Lee, and Jonathan

Ages 12, 19, and 9

I often wonder if the devil was watching me when I was bad. If the devil was watching me, I know God would fight the devil and win.

I often wonder if my first mommy was nice. I think she was taking drugs. I don't think I would like her if I met her now because she took drugs and made me have the virus.

I often wonder what Heaven is like. I think there are angels all over, baby angels and grown-up angels. I also think my friend Cory is there and is happy. When I die, I will see her there. I think I, too, will be happy in Heaven.

Hydeia, age 6

I often wonder what it would be like to never have to take medicine. That would be fun because I would then be able to eat in the morning and when I come home from school.

I wonder what it would be like to grow up and get married. I wonder what it would be like not to have to worry about the shots I get. They hurt, and they sting. I also worry about getting real sick and having to go to the hospital. I really don't like getting needles.

I wonder if I ever will get a four-wheeler.

I often wonder why I always need to take medicine. I wonder why some kids have to take medicine and others do not. I guess I really do wonder a lot.

Justin, age 8

I. Often wonder...
if I will Ever
get rid of hiv.

Tanya
Age 8

with Hiv

without
hiv

happy

sad

I often wonder how often I'm going to get sick and what will happen to me during those times. I worry about how much energy I could lose and if the day would come that I wouldn't be able to play sports or to play with my friends.

I often wonder how much longer in life I have. Sometimes I think I only have months to live. Other times I'm more hopeful, and I think I'll live at least a couple more years.

The thought of not living long scares me. Especially dying. I worry most about what my dying will do to my family. I want them to be able to go on with their lives and not be depressed all the time. In fact, if I was in Heaven and looking down on my family, I would want to see them getting along with each other and remembering me having a lot of fun with my friends always being over.

Kevin, age 13

Kelly, age 16

If only every day was Christmas, then life would be happier (because people are nicer at Christmastime).

If only I didn't have HIV, then I wouldn't have to worry so much about dying.

If only I knew more about what dying was like, then I would probably feel a little bit better about the fact that it might happen.

If only I could talk to someone in Heaven, then they could tell me how it is there, what things there are to do there, and what I should bring.

Rachael, age 9

I Often Wonder...

I often wonder what my life would be like if I didn't have AIDS. I think my life may not have been much different.

But if I didn't have AIDS I would eat more and not be so skinny. I would not have to get needle sticks or take medicine that tastes sick. I would not have to get up at 11pm or at 7am to take medicine and I would be able to eat whenever I wanted.

If I didn't have AIDS I would not have to worry about dying from it. My parents would probably be the same though whether or not I had AIDS. But if I didn't have AIDS they would not have to worry so much about me. It's hard for

me to see my parents worry.

I often wonder how other children without AIDS learn to appreciate life. That's the best part about having AIDS.

By Brett
Age 11

Living with HIV

When You Have AIDS

Hi. My name is Tanya. I have AIDS, and everyone is different than I am. It feels terrible to have AIDS because my tummy hurts a lot and because, if my friends found out, they wouldn't want to play with me. When I told the kids at school I had AIDS, they made fun of me. I told them by accident. Now I want to run away from school. I wish I were not an AIDS patient. I wish I didn't have to take medicine.

When you have AIDS, you feel bad a lot, even when you don't have a high fever. I am different from everyone. AIDS patients hurt a lot. It is going to take a long time to get rid of my AIDS, and by the time I do, I will be too old to live a long while. I'll only live a little while. In the meantime, my friends only understand I have a catheter. They don't understand my AIDS. I wish they would understand. I wish they would be my friends forever.

Tanya, age 6

David, age 14

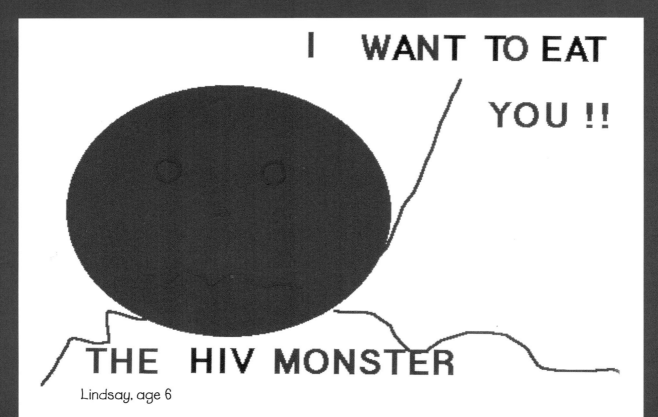

THE HIV MONSTER

Lindsay, age 6

You are about to suffocate me. . . . I hate you because you do
bad things to my body. . . . All you ever do is kill my cells. . . . I wish
you weren't so mean. . . . You are stupid. . . . Go pick on someone
your own size. . . . If you keep killing all of my cells, you are going
to die, and so am I. . . . Get out of here. . . . Leave me alone. . . .
Don't be such a red monster. . . . Let's be friends!

Jonathan, age 9
Sara, age 10

What I Wouldn't Do to Be Normal

Being normal would be like not having to take medicine every day of your life. Being normal is like not having to miss so much school because of being sick and needing medical treatments. Being normal is not worrying every day about if and when you will get sick and about how people will treat you at that time. I would do anything so that I could be normal.

Robert, age 15

It bothers me when...
Doctors wear glove to take an X-Ray

or check you

Jamie, age 13

What It's Like Having HIV

Sometimes you feel sad, and you wish your brother and your sister had it. You don't think it's fair that you've got something they don't. You think, "Why do I have to have it?" but I, B.J., have it.

I wish there was a cure for us that have HIV because we would be well again. I wouldn't have the trouble of carrying this medicine that goes to my heart. Don't you wish that, too?

Some people treat you like you can't do this or you can't do that, and all I want is to do things anybody else can do. Like climb monkey bars or big toys. I want to be normal. Don't you?

This is from B.J., A Friend, age 10

DEAR GOD:
If this was a joke, it wasn't very funny!!!

NOW HIRING A GOD TO HELP FIND
THE CURE FOR AIDS

R.S.V.P. to the world above

Brett, age 12

20

How HIV Really Is

When I first found out about my HIV infection, I was driving in the car with my mother. She told me that I only had six months to live. That is what the doctors told her. She also told me that I would be sick from now on and that I would start losing friends if I told anybody about it. I started crying, and so did she. She pulled the car over and hugged me, but we almost had an accident doing so. That was six years ago.

I did not get to go to school no more because the school did not want me to attend. They got me a home tutor instead. Then, in 1988, I started coming to NIH. The first time was really hard. I stayed there for three months because I was real sick and too sick to start protocol. When I was better, I started treatment and then began coming to NIH every month. All the people that I have met are real friendly and make me feel happy, accepted, and like I have a life to look forward to. I am doing real well, and I am even in school. I feel real hopeful about the future and would love to be a truck driver when I grow up.

It is real hard to get stuck with needles a lot and to know that you may not live long. I get scared going to bed sometimes, worrying that I will not wake up.

For those of you who are HIV-positive, remember to keep God in your heart and to pray every night. Pray for HIV to go away and for everything to be all right for all of us. Pray for people to be more accepting so we can be much happier.

Damen, age 15

Good Days, Bad Days

When you live with HIV, there are definitely good days. Those are the days when I have people who care about me and people who talk to me and make me feel better about my having HIV. Going to the mall with my good friend who knows my diagnosis is fun because this is a day when I don't have to worry about what I say. This is also one of the only days where I don't have to hide in a bathroom to take my medicine. Sometimes I am so tempted to just take out my medicine and take it in front of my friends so they could ask what it was. I could tell them, and I could get this secret over with once and for all. Once I stayed for a sleepover at my friend's house, and I left my medicine in her refrigerator overnight. Her dad took out the medicine and looked up the name in a doctor book but couldn't find out anything about it. He told her not to tell me he did this, but she did, and I felt he was being nosy, and I am not comfortable about sleeping there again.

There are definitely bad days, too. These are the days when the kids talk about AIDS in school and about how they would never touch or go near kids who had it. I once asked a boy what he would do if I had it, and he told me he would never go near me but that he knew that I didn't really have it. He was wrong. I do. And I do have bad days where a lot of things hurt, like my legs, my head, my stomach, my ears, and I see spots out of my eyes.

But the most difficult days are the days when I can't help but think a lot about if I am ever going to get cured. Sometimes when things are going wrong, I think I am not. Most other times when I am feeling well, I know things are going to get better. It is just very hard coming back to NIH when you know that if you make a friend, he may die. My best friend here died. I get scared that the same thing may happen to me. Making new friends is hard because I don't want to lose anyone else who I care about. So sometimes I just get real quiet and stick to myself.

Dawn, age 12

Jamie, age 13

Living with Knowing You Can Die

Everyone knows that you can die from HIV, but no one knows when. Also, no one knows how difficult this is to live with unless you actually have HIV yourself or you love someone with HIV. Living with HIV and knowing that you can die from it is scary. Knowing that you can die is very frightening. I think it is hardest in this order:

Not knowing when this will happen.

Not knowing where it will happen. (I would rather die at home.)

Worrying about my family. For example, will my mother and father ever stop crying? (I don't want them to cry but always remember me riding my pony and being happy.)

What will happen to my stuff and my room? (Casey will probably get most of it, but making a museum would not be such a bad idea.)

Thinking about what my friends will think.

Thinking about dying is hard, but it is good to do because you think about it anyway. Most people don't want to talk about this because it makes them sad, but once you do, you can talk about it more easily the next time. Then you can go on LIVING!

Beth, age 12

B. J., age 9

Family, Friends, and AIDS

Heaven is a very special place. It is special because nothing bad happens to you there. No illness. You get to see loved ones who have passed on.

I will get to see lots of people in Heaven. Like a lot of kids I knew. And a lot of adults, too. That will be really neat.

The hardest part about going to Heaven will be missing people who are here on Earth. Like *my mom*.

The best part is that Mom and I will be together one day, forever.

Jeremy, age 12

Cassie, age 5 (one month after her mother's death)

MY MOMMY'S RAINBOW

Mommy, I want you to know everything. Like how tall I am today, that I did really good with my shot, that I am going home from the hospital today, and that I am starting kindergarten next week. I am going to wear my dress which has flowers on it and is black to my first day of school.

Most of all, Mommy, I want you to know that I miss you and that I think about you all the time. I miss you the most when I am crying. I wish I could fly up there to the sky to be with you. I know that you're not sick anymore, and I hope that you are happy.

(five months after her mother's death)

What it is like to have a
mommy with AIDS!

My mom has Aids, and shes
in the hospital most of the
time, ~~and~~ I don't like it when
shes in the hospital. It scares
me because I never know ~~her~~ if shes
sick or not I don't like it when
shes sick. When shes sick I
never know if she going to die. I
don't like thinking of her
dieing because I don't want
her to die. ~~If she died~~ the
thing I would miss the most is
her kisses and hugs. Right now,
if I could tell my mom one
thing it would be I LOVE YOU!

P.S. I wish you didn't have
Aids and you could be with
us forever. I will love you
forever but if your to tiered to
fight I'll still love you and its OK.

Mara, age 9

The Hardest Thing about All of This

The hardest thing about all of this is *my* brother. My brother is HIV, and he bugs me. He gets a lot of attention, especially when he almost died. Sometimes when he gets a lot of attention, I feel left out. When he gets new toys and Nintendo tapes, I often get nothing. That makes me feel sad. Sometimes I feel angry when *my* mother is busy and can't help me with *my* homework. She is busy with all kinds of activities related to Joey and doing a National Day of Awareness for Children with HIV. I also get angry when I don't have anyone to play with and Joey gets to bring his friends over.

I also get scared. AIDS scares me because I am afraid that Joey will die. I always had a brother, and I don't know how it would feel not to. Sometimes he wants me to sleep in his bed with him. Maybe because he is scared, too. He doesn't talk to me about what it is like to have HIV. But I haven't asked him, either. I told *my* best friend. She told me she would not tell her family, but she did tell them. It worked out OK, and she is still *my* best friend.

If I could change anything in the whole wide world, it would be to get rid of AIDS and that no kids would be sick. I really want *my* brother to know that I love him even if I don't always show it. There are just some times that I have to hit him back.

Lauren D., age 10

My brothers have H.I.V. I have three brothers. They all have H.I.V. It is really hard to see them go throw pain. I Love my brothers alot. I always take care of them when my mom can't. I know that thier not going to die soon, but I'm still scared.

me   Ricky   RANDY   Robert   my mom   my DAD

Candy, age 11

How Important a Job a Sister Has

Being a sister is a very big job. You have to be there for your brothers, share a lot of things with them (especially things you have that they don't), and worry about them.

I worry most about my brother who has HIV. I worry about this in the mornings, in school, and at nighttime. Sometimes I even wake up during the night thinking about his virus. What I worry about the most is that one day he will get real sick, and in no time at all, die. I think that he could die at a young age. I think that he could get very sick and the next morning be so sick that he could not get up and in the next few minutes be dead.

It is kind of scary that he's got this virus, and sometimes you will just blurt it out. Boy, that would be a problem! That is because we are not allowed to tell anyone about the virus because if we did and people found out, they would tell everyone, and then people who don't know much about it could do something mean to us and to my brother.

If I could wish anything at all, it would be that this virus would just go away one of these days. But it will probably never go away. I will never stop wishing, and I will work very hard never to tell anyone about it.

Lauren W., age 7

Marie, age 8

HIV

My Brother has Hiv and I know that he is going to die soon. But I try not to think about that. It hurts me to know that. Cause I love my brother very much. He is special to me and my family they love him too. I hope they find a cure for it real soon.

by Ankeita

Age 11

David
By: Diane

I don't think I could ever be as strong as my brother is. His name is David, and he has AIDS. David has gotten through many hard times, but me and my family has always been there to cheer him on. I think he has become a very strong person inside and keeps on getting stronger with every battle, against the AIDS virus, he wins. Someday I know he won't be able to win a battle, and he'll go to heaven, but that doesn't mean that he lost the battle. It'll just mean that he got tired of fighting. I know I'll miss David when he goes, but I also know that he won't hurt any more. I would like to say one thing to David before he goes, "I love you."

Age 13

me as a spirit

Once my sister got sick on Thanksgiving. She was going to the hospital. Everybody was calling on the phone asking if she was OK. I told everybody she was fine. I said "Hi" to all of them, but no one said anything to me or even "How are you?" The same thing happened on Christmas.

Sometimes I feel like a spirit. I feel like I can be seen but not heard. Not many people pay attention to me. Like a spirit, I am always there, but people don't notice the things I do.

Brianna Keisha, age 10

The Monkey on My Back

I often wonder what will happen to my family because of AIDS. I wish my sister would be all right, but I know she may not be. I wish my mother would start relaxing and not jump to conclusions about my sister so quickly. I also wish my mother will continue to feel well.

I also wish I did not have to lie about my sister's and mother's health. Lying is hard to keep straight, and I wish I could just tell the truth and get the monkey off my back.

Melissa, age 13

Me and My Friends

It is very hard to make friends and to lose them. This is what I remember most about each one of the kids I have gotten to know and love. Jeff loved Rude Dog. He was always nice. Michelle was a cute baby, and she always kept Ernie on her leg. Cory was funny, real nice, and smiled a lot. Ezra was also cute. He had a beautiful face. Aubrey always knew what she wanted and was funny, too.

All of these friends had AIDS. They fought hard to live. Now when I think of them I feel sad, because they had a chance to live but they died, and I knew them all real well. I think they are all in Heaven together now, having a party or something. It makes me feel better to think of them all together because that makes it all seem less scary.

Joey, age 11

How to Treat People with AIDS

One day in class you had said that people who have AIDS deserve to have it. You had been talking about Magic Johnson at the time. Another day you were talking about National Awareness Day, and you thought it was terrible that the gays were there because they were "disgusting" and they should "help themselves." Let me tell you how all of that made me feel.

People with AIDS are just like you and me. They want to live. They do not want to die. They have feelings, too. Comments like you made make people like me have to live in isolation, with no one to know how we feel, what this is like for us. We can't talk to anyone because they might feel the same way you do, and then we would be made fun of, or worse, people would not want us in the school. Yes, I said "people like me" because I, too, have HIV. But you would be the last person I would tell. And you would be the last person to give me support and to allow me to feel that I am an OK person.

People like me who have HIV are scared a lot. We are scared of losing friends. We are scared of getting sick. We are scared of dying. We just want to be accepted and loved like everyone else.

Please think about this. And be careful before you make bad comments about people with HIV. You could not have hurt me more.

Signed,

Dawn

Once your admirer, now your avoider

Age 10

Adam, age 13

What It Is Like When Friends Find Out about Your HIV Infection

When friends find out they ask you all kinds of questions. Like "How did you get AIDS?" and "What is it like to have AIDS?" and "Do you have to take lots of medicines?" and "Is it scary to have AIDS?" I like when people ask, "When are you going to get well?" and say, "I hope you get well soon." The things I hate when people say are "You'll never get well" and "Can I catch your illness?"

I would like for everyone to know that please do not be scared of us—we have feelings, too. It is not so easy to live with AIDS. Be nice, and treat us like everyone else. The worst thing about having AIDS is not knowing if people will be your friends. So please be our friends. We need you to be our friends.

Becky, age 8

If Only

. . . If only my mother and I didn't have HIV, then my whole family
wouldn't have to go through what they have to go through.
. . . If only my dad would be able to talk to us about us being sick.
. . . If only we didn't have to worry so much about money.
. . . If only my mom would stop being so stubborn and start taking
some medicine so that she would not get sick.
. . . If only the world would be a more understanding place.

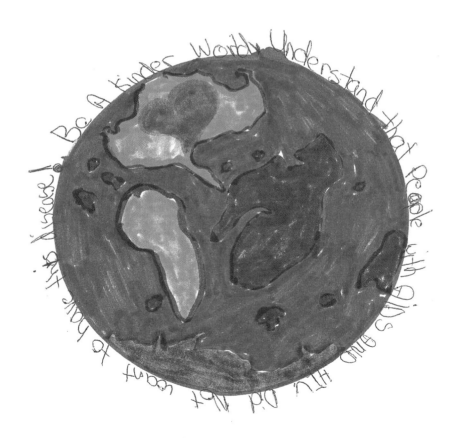

Dawn, age 11